Firebird

Sally Naylor

Poetry Books Press
In support of the Poet

Firebird

Sally Naylor

Poetry Books Press

Poetry Books Press is an imprint of Parson's Porch & Company. Profits from the sale of this books go to support Chattanooga Food Bank.

To order additional copies of this book, contact:

Poetry Books Press
www.poetrybookspress.com
1-423-475-7308

For Grace, Cynthia and Fran

ACKNOWLEDGMENTS

"Caliente" appeared in Texas Poetry Calendar.

"Distant Summer Fires" appeared in Footstep.

"Largo," Key West: A Collection.

"Hiatus," The Panhandler.

"Birding in the Everglades," appeared as "Dichotomy" in *The Panhandler.*

TABLE OF CONTENTS

Preface   13

LANDSCAPES

The Aloe Manifesto   17
Birding in the Everglades   18
Caliente   18
Hiatus   19
Largo   20
For the Birds   21
Sitting a Long Shiva   22
Swimming Through Mountains   24
No Peking   25
For My Students on MLK Day   26
Unsolicited Advice: A Primer on Poetry Revision   27
Anniversary   29
Landscape Maritime   31
Encore   33
Let This Teacher Transcend   34
This Too   35
Expat   36
Runaway Universe   38
Jigsaw   40

SUMMER

A Summer's Notebook   43
For Francis   48

AUTUMN

Blessings: Return to Monterey   55
Jazzed   56
I Will Make My Sleep a Prayer   57

To Hold the Ether   58

After All That Kama Sutra   59

WINTER

Little Things   63

Leaks and Tumbles   64

Providence Gave Me a Skunk   65

It Cheers Me   66

Within   67

Disability Leave   68

Kendra's Happy Birthday Cento   69

Second Chemo   70

Crysalis   71

The Backside of Mowbry Mountain   72

Jack   73

Taking Care   74

Sunrise   75

Creed   76

Exactly   77

Sabbatical   78

Birthday   79

Ode to Myself   80

Valentine   81

SPRING

April Fools   85

Ears   86

The Whole Damn World IV Drip Love Poem   87

Distant Summer Fires   88

In Trance   89

Nectar and Spice   90

There is a soul in me
It is asking
To be given its body.

– Louise Gluck

Preface

SALLY NAYLOR'S *FIREBIRD* IS A REMARKABLE collection of poems in so many ways. Teacher, though she is, and lover of books, Sally's work is never bookish; her poems are spontaneous, not studied. Each time I read them, they startle me with their fresh language, sinuous syntax, and comparisons that are so unexpected yet so right. Of course, the aloe plant would say, "I've re-grown every one of my seven thumbs." How true that the flight of the wood stork is "tender and mathematical as spring." Don't we all want to be tempted "out of the jar for one green hour"? As a poet, I envy such lines; I wish I had written them.

This poet is audacious in exposing her feelings and relentless in tracking down the words to say what she is feeling. Nothing escapes Sally's steely eye in the mirror: battling cancer, losing a spouse, taking a lover, lamenting the loss of a friend, homesickness for other places, other times. She traces the lines of aging in her face and forms from that stark reality "Ode to Myself", a joyous celebration of life.

Sally is closer to Walt Whitman than Emily Dickinson—she sings the body electric in long, limber, luscious lines. She is like Keats, too, in the pagan joy she finds in nature. To read Sally is to see the world—the Everglades, the Florida Keys, Miami, Mowbray Mountain, Chickamauga, Monterey, Manhattan, Nova Scotia—her world, as the poet creates it for us: through words pulsing with the writer's blood, not as it is but as she sees it, "a happy articulation" of her life.

And the reader is the better for it. This subjective vision is why we turn from time to time to poets, after all. The world as it is is never enough. The genuine article has its place and prose its usefulness. But it is the artist's rendering of the real that wakes the soul and, to use Sally's thematic image, stirs the phoenix back to life.

As I see the poet's task, Sally Naylor has said it perfectly:

> Yet hoisting somehow a song
> to the promise of each lunatic morning. . . .
> Then I have only this jumble of syllables,
> this hand, this heart.

As one of her land-locked Tennessee friends, I thank her for helping us "learn to swim through mountains."

—Charlotte Barr

Landscapes

THE ALOE MANIFESTO

Barbed, curled soft, born of light,
nearly invincible. I may languish
in the dark; I may wax yellow or bloat up
from heat or floods,
but just watch – soon I'm back:
healing, reinventing.

I am part Thunderbird, Firebird,
mother to the Phoenix.
Add a pinch of gossamer web,
sunrise, and wolves' teeth to this mix,
for I am light. I create generosity of spirit.
I give when I thrive.

This is the song of Aloe, the song of life.
I am the dance of translucent fluids.
My barbs are soft to the touch.
So go ahead life, tear me up a little,
do your worst.
I come back. I live to give.
I've re-grown every one of my seven thumbs.

Firebird

BIRDING IN THE EVERGLADES

There flies the geometry of Wood Stork
her body a dart in the physics of flight,
all triangles and planes,
her kite-like angularity
an air-piercing, a serious instrument,
a dark argument against clouds.

How delicate her hollow bones,
her feather flutter and soft down,
how prodigious her wing span.
In that white urge she travels, tender
and mathematical as spring.

CALIENTE

for Jose Cabrera

Nostrils flare and eyes tear
as air testifies to the pungency of peppers,
secure in sounds of smooth steel on wood,
in the inexorable chopping of spheres.

Sliced green chilies and tomatoes chopped thin,
then add scallions, a dozen black olives--large,
jalapenos--slice; one soft avocado--dice;
scissor fresh cilantro and sprinkle in.

Finish off this evolving salsa,
this potion of mine, with a bite
of fresh garlic and one dwarf lime.

Accept this offering from my odd kitchen.
An import from alien territories,
a mixture, concocted for its hot delight,
all stimulant and healing,
taken for the burning away of demons.

HIATUS

for Ken

I want to bring you a firefly tonight,

to offer a skittery light show between cupped hands,
to see your vague eyes lit by gaudy blinkers.

I wander through strange yards searching
for elusive, phosphorescent wings.

I remember your early childhood chases,
the capture of neon colonies in a jar
and my maternal lectures on insect sensibilities.

Our compromise--those early morning freeings
of black, lethargic things.

I want to distract you from the dull push,
mitigate your obligations to tutors, books,

to tempt you out of the jar for one green hour.

Firebird

LARGO

You are entering a state of mind

reads the billboard at mile marker three.
Latitude: twenty-four degrees.
New Year's Eve. Fisherman's Trail.

The man who lives with two women
in the stilt house next door knocks
over his beer, cusses out the blonde.

Down in the yard his big black Lab
chases her she-goat, saucer-eyed
with fear, into the chain link fence.

The goat stumbles, harried by the Lab,
its own bleatings, reedy rasps,
wheezings, and the blonde's dry sobs.

No more Bogies and no Bacall.
Neon billboard over the house reads:

Paradise regained: The Florida Keys.

Firebird

FOR THE BIRDS

Blinded by the late December light I went out to shoot some birds
with my Leica,
I'd become a small grey stone without the flux or susurration of oceans,
strung between several poles of an anguish,

I went down to the Everglades of revision. I needed new eyes
and a break from raptors: the harriers and Gyre Falcons of cities.

I needed water birds, delicate waders, the slim elegance of their natures,
and even the fat torpid balancing act of muddy gators, spider lilies,
saw grass, the funny spheres of the curved umber half-moon of turtles.

I needed what I got: that facile darter,
the frail Anhinga airing his laundry wings,
afloat then, in the company of Cormorants.

Voices from Kabul and Baghdad mocked me for suffering; they were right,
so I tucked my little list of dreads into the waxy ocher topknot of a lily.
And then, only avian panoplies:
plump Night Herons, Little Greens, Blues,
Tricolors, the Great Blues,
the White Heron which might have been an Egret.
I consult my Peterson's to check leg colors
then back to scrutinize the plush flutters of Ibis and Glossy Egret.

The dark stones of my eyes soften with sunset into something fluid,
something like flight, or memories of the better part of being human.

SITTING A LONG SHIVA

Of all the laws that bind us to the past the names of things are stubbornest.

--Robert Hass

I miss the élan and glitz. Dan Leslie Bowden. South Beach,
Biscayne Bay, Dante Fascell Park, Fairchild Gardens, Senor Frogs,
Hollywood's Broadwalk, the Anhinga Trail, tourists at Johnny Rockets
in the Grove, even Hialeah and Kendall.
I miss Margery Stoneman Douglas's birthdays and her River of Grass.
Miami, you know I love you, your sweat and chlorine,
your Frangi Pangi alphabet and Villella's ballet.
Ransom Everglades: teaching the pale children of Batista's bodyguards.
No more school years spent wondering who's kin to drug lords.
And no more Santeria scares, no more Brothers to the Rescue.
No more Peer Counseling, no rainbow door or Friends of the Library,
no more fundraising for the AIDS Walk,
no more students who've been kidnapped.
No more Passovers, no more dreidls, no more cantors,
no more Ansins, Obersteins, Servianskys, or Ungers.
No more stone crab, salsa and immigrant stew.
No more hirsute Hassidic Jews.
No more MFA classes at FIU. No more gay queens.
No more gold chains and lavish Quinces.
No more flower vendors. No more children of the stars.
No more Hala Khouri, Mamta Dadlani or Phil Lord.
No more Vilasuso, Echavarria, Pedroso, Valdes-Fauli,
Piedrahieta, Encinosa, or Avila, no more coups.

No more former students like Ilan Arboleda at Publix,
stricken after six years, when I've forgotten his name,
but not his history, his sister at Gulliver School or his mother's red hair.
Into which glossary do such fine ghosts fade?
And just how many countries is it shrewd to lose?
Which atlas will add on a spare room, maybe stutter,
lose its footing a little and finally, throw open its shutters?

Firebird

Miami, I long for your electric chaos and alien cacophonies:
grotesque, hyperbolic, mercurial, over the top, phoenix-like.
How I fit in your flatland of glitter and perpetual loss.
How I need to soothe my own misfit, expatriate heart.
So I'm sitting a long Shiva now,
finished with the memory work and grief, plotting my return and last coup.
I need your tongue, your color, your energy, your cerulean seas.
I need you.

Firebird
SWIMMING THROUGH MOUNTAINS

I'm never sure how to feel in this town of nice blondes
with pronounceable names.
So I soldier on like a seventeen-year-old gone to fight
at Chickamauga. Boredom suggests itself,
which may be a pose that means I can't locate what I need here.

Gone are those ardent lime-green corruptions, the soap operas
and melodramas of hundreds of unpublicized Elian's.
Miami, darling crackpot, your many colored coats, your water birds,
your wild parrots weighing down the Bottlebrush:
the gaudiest gift of a fauvist Christmas tree.
The imbroglios of Spanish moss and insects buzzed electric.
Miami, I miss you.

Such strange trees: Dogwood, Ginkgo, Tulip Poplar.
But on Fridays at the Mountain Opry, in the Bluegrass afterglow
Of *The Orange Blossom Special* Ken Holloway and the Georgia Flaps wind
up with *May the Circle be Unbroken*, and for an instant it feels like enough.
But what happens to the land-locked? I can't know, not yet.
That's the thrill and dry-mouthed dread of it.
Maybe they learn to swim through mountains.

Until then I await the Vladivostok Hun,
the Savior of Krakow, or sweet Jesus of Prague,
the ark or any sort of covenant.
I am waiting for Great Blue Herons
and old stone bread ovens. Until then,
lay me down in sweet swaddling, warehouse or numb me out,
and let me forget, immerse me entirely in magical thinking.

25

Firebird

NO PEKING

Linger a moment in the respite
of the golf course ducks.

Ugly in flapping red flesh
piled atop truculent beaks.
All that plump urgent whiteness
waddling at ambulance tempo
across the fairway.

And, yes, their breakneck plops
shatter the surface of the pond.
No grace of pintail or mallard here.
They're making for the gazebo,
a gathering flotilla,
spread, so that I, like a queen
may distribute my bread
throwing--equitably—one crumb right
the next left
and an extra bit for the small one
right, left, small,
how they need me
right, left, small

and then it is that I am held captive
by the emerald gloss of spreading tail feathers
such unlooked for, impudent fans, fabulous,
like nothing else in Tennessee.

Firebird

FOR MY STUDENTS ON MLK DAY

Black: Black Widow, blackball, black list, the Black Plague,
Film noire, ebony, shady deals, black face, Tar Baby, Uncle Remus,
I Passed for White, minstrel night, pathos, *our darkest hour*, not right.
Pitch, octoroons, anthracite. Take a stand, fight. Darkness,
the Dark Ages, Uncle Toms and the slaves we called darkies.

Colored folks grappling for light. And yes, Medgar Evers,
church bombings, and oh, Dixie, *to live and die in Dixie*.
Like Emmet Till for maybe
whistling at a white woman,
while shadows of a lynch mob haunt
Chattanooga's Walnut Street Bridge.
The Little Rock Nine. The Black Panthers.

Two, four, six, eight, we don't want to integrate.

And what about your granddaddy,
who tells of the assassination: April 4,'68.
That knock on the door and the message: *We got him.*

Cause it's time for the New South,
the Land of Cotton, the Bible Belt,
to stop just reconstructing itself
and to listen to the black and blue music
of its nigras and pickaninnies
it's time for religion to lie down with tolerance.

Swing low, sweet chariot, comin' for to carry me home.

Today in Chickamauga, Georgia men clean confederate tombstones
with strains of *Ode to the Confederate Dead*
not yet mothballed in their heads.
And hey, the guy they call "Duck," acquitted for the '63 beating death
of that Unitarian minister, still sells used cars in Selma
down the street from the Voting Rights Museum.

Look away, look away, look away, Dixie Land.

Firebird

UNSOLICITED ADVICE: A PRIMER ON POETRY REVISION

for Lynda Pinto Torres, Maximo's other grandmother

Turn right into ritual and follow
your rogue your bulldog your greenhorn, your fog.
Verb it! Learn to juggle. Don't rely on carnival tricks – snub the caesura.
It's okay not to know where you're going; you'll never get there anyway.
But just in case you do, you won't be the same, you won't be you.
So either way, pack the fat eraser. Worship process.
Worship tools. Slough off old lives. Play God.
And let there be white space, but let there also be lines.
Don't justify right.

Realize that the mind lies, so set your traps carefully.
Avoid adverbs. Be concise.
Dump that outline and your love affair with the linear and monkey mind.
Then your mistakes will be unlike mine.
Study geography not iconography.

Thumb nose at academy. Don't write the dread chopped prose.
Go home and smash then flutter, your way into startle.
Observe the rule of silence.
Show don't tell. Bucolic beauty just might scoot you on through,
but stitch an ironic frock or two. Play just play. Cartwheel on over.

Embrace the ugly. Study topography. Never write doggerel.
Swoon to the architectonics of your own grand piano.
Unicycle. Scan. Dabble, stack and scramble images. Hyperbolize.
Plant only trapezoids in stained-glass gardens.
Warehouse ambition, exile the ego, don't do confession –
leave that to the masters: Plath and Sexton.

Understate. Stop whining. Get over it. There, there, collage.
Get sticky. Use paste.
Stop thinking. Hallucinate. Embrace the entrails of Frida Kahlo.
Go grotesque.

Firebird

Use color. Draw Dali's bones in Bonsai trees.
Waft them in a surreal breeze.
Goat foot through the restless longing. Fuck the prize. Eschew hubris
or it will do, to you-know-who, you-know-what, too.

So dream. Focus. Bubble up. List. Try origami. Draw with four pencils.
Tear. Cut. Smudge. Catalogue. Read aloud. Don't be cowed.
Finish that book. Start another. Don't rhyme or be redundant.
Ignore advice. Revise. Now look it up. It means to see again.
The red pen, how it never ends. Less is more,
unless it's this, which, by now, should ring true.

Know that I love you and Monty, Max and Elena, Paco too,
and I've forgiven you for writing your Virginia history in prose.
But it might have been an ode. I mean it. It's not too late.

Firebird

ANNIVERSARY

Dear Cathy,

Congratulations, you're off Prozac
but skipped the withdrawal symptoms.
I know that was important to you.
There are other benefits, too: no more bouts
with your shopping addiction or disordered eating.

Today there are eight blooms on your orchid—
the one Park gave me for delivering your eulogy.
You've been in the earth two years now,
and you've missed a lot of suffering.
No one will make fun of your chicken poem
or say you need therapy again.

I bought a pair of those chili-pepper red, Keen sandals,
the original kind, to keep your periwinkle blues company.
It feels odd that your body's out of style but not your shoes.

My act of sedition was a flop.
The bulbs I bought to plant at school, willy nilly,
to commemorate the subversive in you
would be up by now, but I broke my foot this fall.
Remember our golf pro, the one who advised me
against playing with "athletic" you? He never had a clue
that what we were playing wasn't golf.

We were just two girls in a careening cart
collecting pastel balls, teeing up on fairways, breaking rules,
and doing a little animal rescue in between the gossip.
How good it felt to be outside Sunday afternoons,

Firebird

consumed and laughing, the wind in our hair
and sun on our backs. You were a bird in this world,
as Fontaine said—a heron—a Great Blue.

Arms akimbo, your legs stretched on forever
in their long-legged lurch.
You were all angles, girl;
you were hopscotch, jungle gyms, jacks.
You were recess.
You were the metrics of juggling
the calculus of tightrope walking
your little hooded eyes, dark now,
yes, and beady,
the whimsy of your smile curled clever,
curled smart
into that beak of a face.

Shoulders hunched, wings about to emerge,
hands in your jumper pockets,
I glimpse you scooting down the hall some days,
radiant, braced for flight, no more papers to grade.

MARITIME LANDSCAPE

How I keep naming things:
the plump cardboard of egg cartons,
texture of birch bark,
rubeckia along rocky ledges,
places to hide,
to trick the focus
from self's eternal metric,
an anodyne to the mind.
I chant the tidal river, driftwood, stone,
earthen jars, fields of flax, osprey,
nouns with wings.

ENCORE

The night you realize you never dance anymore
is the beginning of the end of marking time
with its interminable loop de loop of work and thing, thing, thing.

You repair to Wislawa
and other Polish poets who know how to cradle grief.
Time now to gather materials for the shroud
woven of silk and something Greek:
yogurt, honey and almonds, perhaps,
woven of surf, bread and olive oil, woven of feathers,
of sage, jasmine, and don't forget spit, pebbles and paste.

Time to lay this epoch in the ground
with a burial more lyric than the life.
Only music will bring you back.

And after the elegies I intend again
to live with myself for the first time
maybe at the beach, with more Flamenco guitar,
more Puccini and Corelli, more Rumi.
I'll hobnob with alchemists and conjurers,
making time only for the adept,
for those who can affix wings,
sing arias from the Song of Songs,
grab me a little grace,
transcend this vale of tears.

I'll Fandango through the paltry,
the "to do" lists,
of this wobbly acorn, this little world,
flirting with death and other insistent resurrections.

Firebird

LET THIS TEACHER TRANSCEND

What summer proposes is simply happiness.
                                        -- Robert Hass

Remember where it all started
the Pacific squalls, the Sierra Nevados,
a creek above Sonora Pass, the raucous jays
and all the orange poppies of your youth and how
you now have to earn each summer
but only after the numb dumb scramble
the paralysis and yellowed refuse of institutions
like mucilage, like manila folders, like Auden's *Silt*
you become what you dread:
a woman who can't find her way to a sentence,
a body that once danced as a three-year-old,
now lurching, itself back to work
a soul that tires in its journey of too many
and too much.

Oh stop
imitating the dying of the people who bred you,
for there are still gazelles and lilacs,
still poetry,
escapades, Beautiful Cove, whiskered harbor seals and beach time
while June holds hands with the daisies.

You have a friend, my friend, and
time yet for planting and a stroll and dipping into books
for word play, chatter and irony.
Hold on for that interval created by if
if I just can make it to summer
where none of this burlesque retains any power.

THIS TOO

My little Corgi, Wakefield, fourteen, is dying.
His hind legs splay out like an A-frame
all noodle legged in their impotence.
they become a tangle of rumpled skin.
At first, it was something
about the right lumbar region of his spine and a tumor.
Now I suspect with the curled hind legs,
it's Degenerative Myelopathy.
Prognosis: several months to three years.
But what good are labels?

His muzzle quivers. I carry him (gingerly) up and
down stairs, take him on short pseudo-walks
thirty paces in the back yard crooning:
Wakie-Doodle, Wake-Dude, Buddy-buddito,
dog–in-the-world, going for a walk.
He gets more treats and the leftover smoothie juice.

On his small haunches
sits my marriage of thirty-four years,
also dying, also splayed, hunched, tangled.
At sixty-four the lines of my face
and folds in my neck testify to it all.
One of the spoiled darlings of my culture,
I have tried to love and worked long and well.
And yes, I can bear these losses,
there is some space here,
and I'm holding it (gingerly) in the light.

EXPAT

I.

But what about the angle of the late afternoon sunlight suffused through the gothic window in my new 1798 house, and that sheen on the wide-beam softwood floors, shining like a giddy virgin? The truest sense lies in the collaged moment: dust motes in the air, the old rocker, these shards of now, juxtaposed sunlight and reflection, the layered air, here, another somewhere, seeking the life I failed to live.

II.

But this is also from another life, that first life, before I discovered the virtue of excavation and matches and the advantages to going backwards to exorcise histories and the trick to un-steaming the image before the mirror. Before I released. I am now more deconstruct than con. It's old Penelope's unweave; it's a holy unravel. It's not about building a case, theses or sense. I did believe in having a voice once until I stacked too many images, believed my own fiction, rode the surge of collective mythology and the tower fell. Call it Babel. Call it Hell. Poets creating narratives can't tell a word from a window or a clapper from its bell. And who cares anyway? It's only language.

III.

At the farmer's market in Annapolis Royal, a violin serenades the bustle of bodies amid buckets of lupine, sunflower and gladiolas. Rows of onion, beans, beets, garlic, are presided over by the garrulous white-bearded vendor in all the tourist brochures as he greets me with herbs and pesto recipe and $7 tomatoes. It's my first Saturday, and I locate a wooden high chair for my grandson, Max, procure bags of organic ginger, dark chocolate and drink in the sky of this hard air, the salt water, the wharf, as smells of steak and kidney pie waft across from the pub. A profusion of women traipse by in sensible shoes. And I consider this place. The weathered hexagonal barn, the Queen Anne B&B, the dykes, the concerts, the street dance, potteries, antiques, the gay couples, the ruddy Scots, the Nova Scotian artist's co-op at Bear River. What does it all mean? Home by noon, I put in two rows of lettuce, hang clothes on the line and stack beach rock smoothed by the Fundy shore. A summer expatriot, exulting in it.

RUNAWAY UNIVERSE

The dim red lines of super novas
suggest that Einstein's cosmic constants
were not his consummate blunder but right on,
according to the British PBS commentator.
With gravity losing its grip in an uncanny acceleration,
it's a runaway universe;

we become all whoosh and expansion;
enter the concept of dark matter.
Studies of white dwarfs and super novas,
some fifty million light years away,
lead us to the concept of dark energy;
defined as a small constant force stretching the universe, if it is there.

And then the scientists, one of them like a boy
you might have played Red Rover with,
someone you can trust,
someone who dreams,
he says that this repulsive trip
at the end will give us nothing to see, no other galaxies,
not even a planet or two. Alone.
Only the earth pummeled forth
into dark matter and dark energy, and that's it;

it could be a metaphor, if they are there, if they are both there.
He says it creeps him out.

And so at the University of Michigan with its scientific balloons,
duct tape and grad students,
they measure the energy and try to be casual,
but the pie is full.
Full of nothing as we get closer

Firebird

to the expanding gift of dying stars.
I don't really understand, but I'm scared;
it sounds too familiar, this flying apart

this dark matter and energy, that movement away from, yet towards,
how we do it every day, how we do it together, how we do it alone.

JIGSAW

I shall get you put together again
someday
after my sentence is up,
and the rage turns to smolder,
I'll reassemble this odd geometry
of sky, elbow, and skin.

Summer

Firebird
A SUMMER'S NOTEBOOK

1

FOR RON

I crawled into the high, narrow bed
of your dying and held you,
so wizened,
so not the guy who hiked Canadian mountains
who hefted bags and babies for me.
How I loved your vigor, your CBC voice,
your Library of Congress gig,
your calm, your body loving my body.
Now it has come to this. Ash.

2

The school secretary from Red Bank High
cried on the phone today
when I told her you had died.
An hour later the message arrives
confirming the last (I hope) of your post mortem financial lies.
It is hard to hear.
So on Tuesday the boys and I deliver eulogies
and the next Monday I sign the dismissal of divorce papers.
You are the bittersweet that never untangled.

3

GRIEF

I could go on about the memorial service, but it was perfect and over.
I could focus on insurance claims, annuities, medical bills

Firebird

or death certificates, but I just got in my car and headed south.

In New Smyrna Beach, I find I can't meet my best friend's eyes,
and I'm afraid of the ocean for the first time in my life.
In Delray Beach I cry on my yoga mat for an hour and a half.

Later, walking, I fall to my knees, hands raised
and ask for grace from Baba-ji, prince of light,
ask for the grief to go away, and it recedes.

The evening is temperate
with a light mist and the expanse green, the sky large
and I walk over a hill to observe a lake
and spot what looks like a turtle
by the water's edge and a kind of joy possesses me
until I note the stillness and bloated body
and hear myself yelling,
Don't be dead. Don't be dead.

It was a dirty trick, a fuck you,
a God-hates-this-woman-moment.
The message: this is all you can expect,
death served up after death. It is still June.

The next day I spot a coral snake on the sidewalk.
Knowing this is something I can believe in,
this slim, ringed toxic circumference,
I throw pine needles and cones at it.
I want it to take me. Life is a viper.

Firebird

4

Not even the statue of St Gregory
with the gecko on his head
can stop the strangler fig working its way up the courtyard pine.
It seems unkind to celebrate its splendor.
I also judge and avoid the vulture, leech and bottom feeder.
Which is worse, being the parasite or being sapped by it?
And what does this have to do with marriage
Is there a symbiosis that respects other organisms?
Can I do it? Will I know it when I see it?

5

SOUTH BEACH

At Pita Spice I order the Shawarma sandwich,
two pounds of lamb and joy,
while the boys in the kitchen check out Ataturk Stadi,
the 2003 soccer highlights. Another Turkish delight.

The guy with the albino python is out
sharing his reptile
as a woman in four inch wedges
and substantial Jello breasts wobbles
her bike down Ocean Drive.
Coconut palm fronds dance in the salvation
of a strong breeze as parrots screech cacophonies.
A buff guy on roller blades darts down the street.

Firebird

6

Like some newly soothed nymph,
I pick up shells with my feet.
I bobbed and then floated in the surf,
with white, land-locked toes two feet higher
than my head
as the wave reaches its crest and scoots me
down its undulating spine.
I know the ease of fluid, its silken lace,
my skin pinking with sunlight, I want to say: join me.

7

FOR KEN

At the airport with the ocean still in my mouth,
I order flan and Key Lime Pie with mango juice,
holding onto the last bit of sweetness
before returning to stand on my own two feet.
I don't know why I'm crying, son,
except that maybe Miami and your time and love,
they just do this to me.
The birthday was yours: the gifts were mine.

8

So I used to ride a motorcycle and smoke a ladylike pipe;
it's that sort of impulse, that *born to be wreckage forever* thing.
That's why I write – which is a lie – I write because I'm driven.
And it's tumbling out faster than I can catch it now –

closer to dictation than composition.

9

I crawled all year and then dragged through June and July,
who knows? Maybe I'd always crawled.
Maybe it was always more dark and tunnel than spark.
But when I learned to breath, the ashes cooled,
the architecture of my body shifted,
and I forgot what it meant: trying to please.
I'm retiring now to woo distant parts of myself.

10

My work is to remember who I am
and treasure those glimpses
even when the stout Cuban woman
starts to clean up the ocean and throws batches of seaweed my way
or when the clueless guy playing water football
splashes salt water in my eyes. To remember who I am
even as the German tourist's carry-on slams into my face.
My job is to be here, ferreting out the perfections.

11

DIRECTIVE

Dear Madame Hustle, aka Ms. Impatient or my chum compulsion,
So busy, busy, busy: they didn't move fast enough
for you yesterday at Office Depot did they?

Can you give it a rest? Open and relax, breath, float like the lotus?

Firebird

There is nothing left -- absolutely nothing
you haven't fought or resisted.
So drop your damn plans and just be. Flow. Let go. Release.

Firebird

FOR FRANCIS

I.

At the San Francisco airport I was arrested
the day after we met by a painting, *Homage to Zane Grey*
in all its juxtaposed cartoon-colored Bay Area Funk:
dark green Manzanita, coyote, pine, boot, sky,
its beauty waiting for me to want to give it to you,
and next to it, the metallic sculptures,
those polychrome boys cantilevered across the wall
shining like an angel or truck driver, like your rendition of *Peggy Sue*
or the thing itself, the one: me, you.

I wanted to weep for art in public places
but never could trust a poem that cries.
So locate your guitar
and accept instead this squiggle from the boundaries of lust.

II

POST-TRAUMATIC EUSTRESS SYNDROME
F
I've recovered from your resume,
your rigidity, your honesty,
the music of your DJ voice
even my own colossal naivete.
But I still flash back to the unbearable joys
of our Monterey epiphanies
and then the physical electricity
but feel no loss, have sought no treatment.

Firebird

I sip it all now like a fine tea:
the beauty, the memory.
Nothing real can be lost, so I'm letting it be.
I hope you are well
in that six-foot plus, rogue, Manhattan version of me.
S

III.

YES
I want to hold your face in my hands
And share your laughter with my eyes.
I can see you wearing the nifty vest you bought for Korea.
and your bald head giving me directions
again. I feel your judgment and my resistance.
Yesterday in Barnes & Noble, when I turned into the poetry section
I like how poem after poem reminded me of your hand
against my back, steering me through the Harleys,
kitsch & crowds of New Hope, Pennsylvania.
I was hungry for love then. Incessant.
I cried when the crumbs were gone.
I'm allowing for you to change your mind. Also
I'm allowing myself a beach on which to meet a stranger.

IV.

You gave me several words,
and after they unfurled, I floated.
Like a feather on a pond,
I trace the rhythm of that moment,

Firebird

the thrum of its mouthing,
the lucidity of its tug.
Vivid as mercury,
it will never be clearer.
This is what I want.

Delirious to hear it again for the first time,
I make it my mantra,
my tongue rolling it around
the echo chamber of my mind,
like a frolic, like a bomb: "Good night , darling."

V

How is it you smell of the slash pines of Florida?
How is it that your body is the long tendril
that tethers me to August, to this earth,
you are rain, sea grape leaf, the sun's dazzle.
I want to burrow into your arms and chest and shout
yes, beauty, yes. You are taproot.
I become half mammal, half hibiscus.
Savor my prodigal sugars.

VI

I'd like to transport a whole chorus of Tennessee frogs and crickets
out of my woods tonight, singing their simple leafy, grass and twig lives
full of thrum and glory – whole, like only hundreds of thousands
in concert can be. I'd haul the entire symphony up to New England
for you and your BMW biker guys

where they'd perform arias
and other high operatic gestures
as you settle down to sleep,
for the cricket sings, as do you, with its whole body,
from apertures, wings and spindly legs to fringed feet.

VII

Dear Fran,
Our love affair may collapse; death, pestilence, and desertion exist,
but now I'm on the plane reading my poetry
besotted with words and our stories
trying to archive it
but mostly obsessed with the romance of futility
the reading and writing, reaching and living,
not really caring if I get anywhere but now,
that is key, to say what can't be said,
and nothing and no one can take that from me.

And when my mind settles on you,
I feel your hand on my shoulders
steering me away from moving cars in parking lots
or the tug as you pull handfuls of my hair.
I see us dancing to Buddy Holly
and listening to street musicians as you sing along
in your Manhattan C&W twang.
And then the carousel and being carried to bed
and afterwards being wrapped in your arms.
Can it get any better? So far, always, it has.

Autumn

Firebird

BLESSINGS: RETURN TO MONTEREY

So this time I discover you are just a boy, that you are shy.
I note the occasional tentativeness, how brave you are,
and I love it more than your resume or East Side banter.
You have new poems to give as I consider
the ribald lyrics to the C & W song you are composing,
on demand, for me. You are well into the second stanza
of your low-down, dirty twang, singing with our levitating bed.

*

Maybe I'll get it right. I'd like to learn
how to love myself and then another.
I want a team, a comedy routine, a duet, some sort of male twin.
Joy and tolerance will be our only duties.
Then we'll invite the whole world in and cut them a slice of our blessings.

*

Goodbye again to Pebble Beach, to Carmel, to azure,
to Asilomar's dunes, twisted pines, scrub jays, deer and raccoons,
and the light shimmering on the pacific.
Goodbye to no such thing as land-locked.
Goodbye to last week's ecstasy and last year's epiphany and pain.
Goodbye to gratitude, a great prologue for the next chapter.
This, at last, is replete. Goodbye. Hello and Happy Anniversary.

JAZZED

As I join your half-morphed mischief,
love is the guitar in your voice,
your kvetching Yiddish and mock British;
it's your chameleon.

It's the bridge your body extends to mine
and the after hush, like the low trill of doves
or the candlelight of our blessings.

How like a wordless prayer
the future we nurture opens.

Our love is a verb of being and action.
It's a smooth yes, a magnet,
the polarities pulse: primordial, symbiotic, seminal,
jazzed with electric possibilities.

Firebird

I WILL MAKE MY SLEEP A PRAYER

to the gifts of time and journey
and your generosity,

wanting the grace to fit into the puzzle of how you love
while I rip old paper from my walls

reaching for respite, burdened with memento and fear
that I'll ruin it.

Yet hoisting somehow a song
to the promise of each lunatic morning.

And what can I give you for thanks?
I can give myself back to myself.

Then I have only this jumble of syllables,
this hand, this heart.

TO HOLD THE ETHER

So how do we bear such longing?
Only with the knowledge that we are one,
that I am you, that there is, against all logic, zero distance.

I carry you with me chanting perpetual mantras.
I mouth your name reciting our memories
like a nun at her beads:

devout in the jackhammer of California woodpecker, epiphany and surf,
your rendition of *Peggy Sue,* your tree, then later, the bridge at New
Hope, how I loved you that golden day, and the marathon that was
Atlanta, how it almost crippled us, how you called me kiddo on the way
to the airport, the losses, the grief, *the iron circumstances of the world*,
the resurrections, the new hope, the Tennessee carousel and sculptures,
dancing to Buddy Holly, 1381 Embers, our anniversary, photos, twelve
o'clock , your purloined twine and Boy Scout knots, a feather, our music,
our music, our sex, our muse, incessant fervor, this fever, I love you, this
rush, the need to make it eternal, to hold the ether , so hopeless, so
exquisite, so over-the-top, so impossible, so potent, so fluid, so possible,
so heady.

So just how do we bear such longing?

Maybe it's our gift –

a way to extend, to prolong the beauty of touch,
how it must be dissected, memorized, rehearsed.
I love you. And then rewound, our geographies
studied, mentally caressed and incubated for a month

till we get (I love you, can I say it enough?)
to do it "live" again.

Firebird

AFTER ALL THAT KAMA SUTRA

time, the heat and shudders,
then the cuddling hours on the couch
by the light of the fireplace,
after sharing, "Skimpy," a collaborative piece,
we soak together in the tub
perfection stacked on perfection
the universe lavishing us with gift, gift, gift
as I arch my back, and you swish water over me and stroke my breasts,
your words hit like something false or shattered,
"So what is this?"

Then we probe and knead the lump,
that one marble-sized mass transforming the world
into my mother and grandmother, Cynthia and Grace,
and their mutilations.

Fear came first, and then the gratitude that you were there
to find it, and then the other gratitudes,
coming faster now, how you sat with me saying, "one step at a time"
through days of waiting, then waiting rooms and procedures:
sonogram, mammogram, diagnosis: cancer, all of it together.

Before you had to fly home you reminded me to breathe,
you held my feet during the medieval biopsy
and later my hand in the hospital cafeteria.
I'm typing in the Beijing Olympic shirt you left behind.
You deserve better. I deserve better.
Somehow, I'll beat this. Just watch me.

Some have said I'll get through this.
Only you have said
we'll get through this.
It reminds me that what we need is not
so much to be celebrated but to be united
and someday you too

Firebird

or I will vanish into the unreachable distance
unless we are blessed enough to go together,

but today my heart just aches
to have you hold me with your real arms,
not your imagined limbs,
the phantoms I weave around myself each night
to help me sleep.

Winter

Firebird

LTTLE THINGS

You tossed me a present
as we left for my surgery at 4:30 am,
that twenty year calendar,
so like you -- turning it into a joke.

How cozy in purple socks and heated
lavender surgical gown, how balloon-like and warm
despite the few thin, quick, sentinel node needles,
and then how you helped me focus
as we negotiated
with the anesthesiologist
and lost, but it didn't matter
since she listened
and talked us around.

I never knew
when they gave me
the knock-out drops
just that you were there afterwards
and so were my lymph nodes.
Little things.

LEAKS AND TUMBLES

My heart is too full.
Stuffed with love, it mambos,
leaks and tumbles onto the carpet,
swirling me above the stats, the DFS's:
disease free survival rates, of this hospital of a world.
I never noticed how we are all dis-eased and dying, until now
Yet I am love. I am being love. I am in love. I am loved.
Take it all and multiply, then square it,
And voila! You've biopsied my heart.

Firebird

PROVIDENCE GAVE ME A SKUNK

which I stalked from dumpster to dumpster last night.
I was agog with the rotund fluffy stripe
and the luxury of the flag of a tail wafting lazily,
and my good fortune to meet this mischief maker;

I trailed it for three blocks from the hospital dining hall
through the dark alleys of Zion, Illinois.
We were two scavengers,
flaunting our own brands of pluck and plunder,
sorting through so-called garbage.

Too long, I relied on intellect, denied the mysteries,
avoided flotsam and jetsam, until I grew a tumor.
And that's what it took,
that and the time for reverie.

So I'm glad to have stopped killing myself
working so hard at rational.

I'm arranging a carnie show now, a bone dance,
of bandanas, hats, false eyebrows, scarves,
turbans and a brace of faux bangs.
I'm stepping out – gaudy as a dumpster skunk.

Firebird

IT CHEERS ME

when you take the time to call before my flight,
and I can chatter about my caretaker adventure:

the thirty year-old blonde surgery discharge, a teacher,
who had much pain and no money.
She was dropping things on the hospital shuttle bus,
so I gathered it all up and bought her some Advil
and lined the pills up next to the water.
I put her to bed, and she told me she needed this
since she always takes care of others,
that she had nothing left to give.
It was ministering to myself.

Thank you for sharing my life.
I am not lonely, Manhattan,
even though I'm writing
from the Great American Bagel Bakery at Chicago's O'Hare,
even though we've shared less than a month
of each other's company
even though I'm flying home,
even though we will still have the nothing
that is almost a thousand miles between us.

Firebird

WITHIN

So I'm alone on New Year's Eve conducting Handel's *Messiah*
with my imaginary baton.

It's the third day after chemotherapy.
I am silken, a kind of ribboned ecstasy

floating beyond time,

I'm aware of challenge,
the barbs beneath,

but in this ethereal space -- I banish it all.

This silk has the feel of lovers lying together;
it's that kind of ease yet scintillation.
Something at the core of things just emanates peace.

I'm high on my solitude, the chorus,
and who wouldn't love the violins,
the tenor's tremolo, the crystal air,

my flickering fireplace,
the fog outside, and the god who flies within.

Hallelujah!

DISABILITY LEAVE

Days fold into one another as I putter.
I stop making lists.
Without them I forget what to worry about.
Days accumulate:
Hanukah, Christmas, New Year's, my first chemo,
and then today: day twelve:
the nadir.
How soon and how lightly
ten pm creeps upon me.
And what have I done?
Run a few medical errands
And let friends feed me food and empathy.

I go crazy when I lose five-sixths of my white blood cell count.
Was I a bitch? I can't remember. I faint twice in public places.
Dizzy. I'm a top at the end of its twirl -- ready to topple.
The sky, everything,
falling.

I read and write tirades and take myself off email,
then I'm too tired to care.
Lesions, infections and digestive malfunctions, multiply, rotate,
return like the geese,
a new symptom and medication every ten hours.
Side effects exacerbate side effects.

But now either it's a good hour or I'm numb to it.
I'm ok with the quiet, and with my phone, I'm not alone.
I relax into the slow lack of external pressure as the days stack up.

Firebird
KENDRA'S HAPPY BIRTHDAY CENTO A LA RUMI

So my dearest sparkler, sprite, svelte sophisticate, buddy,
just because I cried on my thirtieth birthday
(I thought I was old) doesn't mean you should. Have more sense.
Or cry and laugh at your tears. I was older then than I am now.
So don't grieve. Anything you lose comes round in another form.

My advice is "What other people think of you is none of your business."

And don't forget to *forget the world and so command it.*
Be a lamp or a lifeboat or a ladder.
Help someone's soul heal.
Stay in the spiritual fire. Let it cook you.
Give yourself a kiss, and if you live in China
don't look somewhere else, in Tibet or Mongolia.
Since the world is a blind man squatting on the road
live in the nowhere you came from
even though you have an address here.
Hear the blessings, like blossoms, dropping around you: God.

Sally

SECOND CHEMO

It hits hard at two pm the second day.
The plug has been pulled.
I drain away.
My skin stinks of metal.

The toxic waste dump I've become
is no stranger to old grief, New Year's grief
anticipatory birthday grief, February grief and March grief,

I look out over the rubble.

"They" say I'll go downhill for the next thirteen days.
Maybe I'll crawl into the darkness I came from:
 mouth open, bald, staring into space.

Sometimes I pretend to be alive
to make others feel better.

But death, I think, must be better than this.
I'm tired of being miserable and telling lies,
and it hasn't even been twenty-four hours.

CRYSALIS

Today, again in the sun,
I sort of cascade beyond myself:
become the pond across the street,
the sleeping dog, the grubs in the pine bark –
bulging -- ready to break out – in two months.

But by then I will have traveled so far,
dropped so many fears
and their mutant complications,
by then
suffering will have become my amnesiac friend.

Firebird

THE BACKSIDE OF MOWBRAY MOUNTAIN

Montlake Road is closed due to mudslides.
I read CAUTION: Logging Trucks Entering
and get another clue
as to why this is called Hot Water Road.

The switchbacks on this creosote ledge with no shoulders
induce a sort of vertigo. My romantic life is a Hot Water Road.

Two men propose to spend the same weekend with bald me.
I've decided it's not my job to make this decision. It will make itself.

An old lover phones daily; together we exorcise my chemo blues,
a respite from the hard-driving, dazzle of the long
physically absent, lately working, lately busy, lately something Francis,
who supports me whatever I do, excepting whining.

So I'll let it be what it wants. What counts isn't really the plot
or even the impulses that propel it.

And yes, I do prefer fidelity,
but I'm an in-betweener now,

so I'm trying to get out of my own conventional way,
to get back to knowing myself, if I can find her,
to let romance come if, how, and when it can
as this becomes the book I'm not writing.

JACK

for Byron Katie

Yesterday the Jack Russell Terrier in me circled
and lay down,
and then again tonight,
I breathed exquisite peace
after my rabid fit and extended pain.

I looked directly,
asked the questions,
then deflated,
the logic
stood upside down.
My thoughts let go of me.

It was a release
ludicrous in its simplicity,
a kind of exorcism: a truce.
I love you Jack. You could do with some sleep.

Firebird

TAKING CARE

Waking late,
I play with turbans, scarves and bathing suits
anticipating Miami with Francis
during the "good" week of my chemo cycle.

Stirring two scoops of Immune Quick Start in V-8,
I count pills,
then chop and mix hard-boiled eggs
with lemon pepper, mayonnaise and Greek olives.

I toast French bread with garlic butter,
layering it with two slices of Boston lettuce
and pile the luxury of egg salad on top.

I reheat my slice of steak and six stalks of asparagus
finishing off with a small glass of milk and pumpkin bread
with liberal lashings of butter.

I consider worthy projects

but am drawn to a patch of sunlight
on the rug next to the fireplace,
so I lie down in its warm center and purr,

building lunch in my head:
chowder with clams, tilapia and scallops.
Spinach salad with feta cheese and pumpkin seeds.

Everything is perfect the way it is.

SUNRISE

I celebrate the concoctions
of our minds,
the interplay, the roller
coaster, the puns,
and feisty argumentations.
Your facile dance of persuasion.

I love your Madison Avenue ad man self
and how my baldness reminds you
of the young (so discreet) Dalai Lama
and how you call me "your monkness"
and say, "Hello, Dalai."

How you say we now share the same barber.

I enjoy your logical explications
and how I jumpstart myself to keep up,
settling back into my sleepy southern habits later
to listen to my own intuitive self.

Like the spun-gold notes Chanticleer
rackets at first light, we're a happy articulation.

CREED

I say yes in red to you
in a fever, a flush
yes, in the thrust and gallop of heat,
This is that yes
from a mouth awaiting its harvest.
You are my green bed
and the pulse of my sex and sleep.
You are the sentinel of my dreams,
end of exile,
my voice, my creed:
love without loss.
Mist, sunrise, sea breeze.

EXACTLY

You are exactly the man I wanted
to teach me about love. But are you perfect? No.

I could catalogue your foibles, but
this is really just to say, you have the pizzazz,
the savoir faire, the mind, the unstinting optimism,
the voice, the size 13 shoes, the long, going-on-forever body parts.

You are all the best sounding flowers:
foxglove, forget-me-not, everlasting.

You are the antlers of the renegade buck,
winged tenacity or simple courage
tap-dancing its way
through this turn-coat life.

You are the alien, the male,
I find myself mirrored in.
You are the first love poems I am meant to write.

SABBATICAL

I invite you to get out.
Go sit in Central Park.
Leave your work and workshop.

I invite you to soften
and let loose thoughts lap your shores
and burnish all edges as they bubble up.

Re-create a sabbatical space.
Give up rock and roll for lullaby
at least for a while.

Unfettered, cradle yourself as I would
for one cloud-like hour.
Feel my lips and fingertips on your eyebrows and temples.

I invite you to trade in guitar and drums
and locate a flute, become a warbler.

Let the dandelions salute
that lark of your newly soothed life.

BIRTHDAY

As I wake

a woman kisses my lips, cheeks, forehead.
I am that woman.

I slip deep down beneath the covers,
raise my knees,
spread my legs, and give birth to myself.

I'm all infancy: bald, soft, blurred vision,
sweet with the scent of my own milk.

I was trained not to talk of such things,
but today I belong to myself.

ODE TO MYSELF

I delight in your skin suit,
that svelte silken vest,
and the swivel and sway of fluid hips.

And girl, I adore the rise and
fall of your still giggling breasts;
don't forget the dark circles
under eyes set in a clown's face.

I dig you compact, slim,
how you were made to sprint.

I love you curly, straight and without a hair on your pixie head.

And your soul trip, I savor it most, morphing
from mortal to infinite -- ten times a minute.
The dandelion, willow, the granite and redwood in you,
I salute them too.

I relish how you take – with both hands -- ripping out the roots.
I fancy how you open, how you soothe, how you lend a hand,
how you age, the cartoons and melodrama you create.

I'm partial to the crow's feet and scars, your lines, and Buddha belly.
I'm nuts about your lop-sided smile,
attitude and wry wit, your lawyer's hat,
your chock-full mind -- ruminating beyond your body's stamina,
how you never have time, how there is never enough.

You're insatiable. I celebrate your lust, impatience and feist.
I love you, Sally. You are my god. You know how to play.
Kaleidoscopic, dazzled, a symphony of appetite, a new story each day.

Firebird

VALENTINE,

take care of your heart—
the whole, bold, exuberant, erotic clarity of it.

I have nothing to give you today but love –
I give it with my body
and with the pulse of words.

I give it in silence and from great distance and no distance.
Steady as a metronome. Yes.
You are the heart of my heart.

I want you to be and do what you want.
I trust you to do exactly what you'll do.
I also notice I have no choice.

And as I learn and relearn this, I glimpse my freedom.
You are my gift.
So I'll be keeping myself too as I join and rejoin you.

But in those spaces when I forget to remember myself,
it soothes and delights me to have found you again,

for we are Nijinsky
in the moment
leaping beyond gravity
falling like a feather
in a swoon of grace.

Spring

Firebird

APRIL FOOLS

I have your handprint traced and stuck with magnets on my fridge,
with Max written crookedly across the palm.

We play Easter egg, cry baby, and high five games with him.
And maybe I do make paper airplanes like a girl
but after four-year-old Max and the family leave,
as we walk along the river holding hands,

how you keep reaching for me,
how we were hungry for more than hot chocolate and biscotti.

How our appetites spark
and leave our skin
savoring cool spring breezes and bird song
as we fall asleep upstairs.

Nights you swaddle me in well-muscled arms.
We do so much nothing. And we do it well:
a little dancing, some photography, an art gallery,

later, your tongue no stranger to greed,
my lips delicious with pink screams.

Firebird

EARS

As I wrestle with my mind about your absence,
how long, after all, can we live this way

and maybe some other emotions
which flit about the outskirts of jealousy

a little fear, perhaps,
some
I –am-not-worthy thing kicks in

and then some
where-is-my-courage stuff?

Meanwhile the sun shines
on the green plush on the hill
as I sit warmed by my heating pad
wrapped around the IV tubing
in this clinic full of Georgia folks
exuding combustible politics, pretty "mannuhs,"
the one True God,

and hopeless, hopeless,
I can only love them all,
you, myself. Snapping my fingers
I say, "Here mind, good mind,"
stroking and scratching its silken ears.

Firebird
THE WHOLE DAMN WORLD IV DRIP LOVE POEM

Hey, get this: lotus blossoms unfurl from my ears.
I celebrate. My mind is still, breath smooth and even.

Reckless with a love that could name the sky,
a love that wants the other to have everything,
that doesn't need for herself, has no ego, façade, defense,
becomes more, always more, when joined.,

I love Tennessee, Miami and Nova Scotian neighbors,
family, former students, Jill's acupuncture, Reiki,
and Melissa who injects B-12 at the Baylor clinic,

I whisper, I love you. I love you Sally. I love you cancer,
friends, colleagues, and the Cancer Treatment Center of America,
I adore my guides and releasing communities.

I cherish Fran and my two other self-appointed male midwives.

Such generosity: food, cards, paintings, piano compositions,
food, phone calls, flowers, dog sitting, food, choreography,
cups of tea, help releasing, food, prayers and sympathy.

I even love surgery, the ER, chemotherapy:
Cytoxan & Taxotere, fatigue, thrush, staph
and the two other infections,
tears and fear, I cherish you, too,
along with Dr. Valle and his jolly "torture chamber,"
Doc Adams's clinic and Michelle's hyperbaric,
Faynette's ozone sauna and lymph treatments,
my hand bruised from the IV,
and Jackie who prays every time she sticks me.

Firebird

DISTANT SUMMER FIRES

I watched Watts blaze from a custom-made convertible
in Palos Verdes Estates, then the forest fires up at Big Bear,
and finally, on TV, the self-immolation of the priests.

I shook my head over the whole gone green world of mountainside.
Shamed at my confusion over the lights of Watts aflame;
it felt weird as Rome and Nero, but awe argued with disgust in my belly,
for the monks, shaven, their tiny pin-heads,
quaint look-alikes for St. Joan, and I want to say Elmo, too, his fire.

It's then that I remember, John, my movies brother,
working his way up to art director; a non-union man then,
no health insurance, burned on the set, in an explosion.
The ambulance, finally, and early morning physical therapies,
the daily scraping, the tearing off of newly healed skin,
his ordeal, flushed out in my own head--years ago now.

Time is the fire in which we burn, said Delmore Schwartz,

who came to such a sorry end. But John today--healed.
Yet, still a kind of Marshall McLuhan media moment.

How he returns to the movies, religiously,
calling like Goethe for *more light, more light*
as he puts together deals, scorched by the old flame, grimacing,
eager to make art and money, how like a priest transcending pain.

And now I'm the one, the firebird, bald in my monkness, burned first
by the surgeon's knife, then chemo, and next radiation,
the body electric, learning to love it.

IN TRANCE

To be empty to be full to pray.

To look for doors, windows and construct hinges, escape.
To remember who I am in the dark.

To be empty to be full to pray.

To travel lightly and kindly, to shed skins, to slough off
to skip, to dabble in halcyon days,
stringing it all together,
to spin, to infinitive, to not split, to word play
to circle, to gyre, to spiral or eclipse.

To center, to warp, to woof, to weave.
To wide-eye with wonder, to paint,
to polychrome with color, to mold clay, make art,
to return it all to white space, to reverse to
enjamb, to reverberate. To have a voice, articulate,
meditate, to empty, to be full, to make art.

To be empty to be full to pray.

Two embrace, to bull leap, to absorb and penetrate.
To male, to hard rock, to reverberate,

to milk, to name, to have and to hold—this horizon,
this fire rising, this flight into a flight into day.

NECTAR AND SPICE

Our bodies may be temporary,
like fireworks,
but that doesn't make it any less beautiful
as they explore our nectar and spice world.

For the after-effects of loving
there is no antidote,
but I'm a little phoenix–smug today
fresh from the ashes
with all this extra space and light.

So I say to my heart: compose,
and to my body: stretch and lift,
and to my mind: get used to it. Look directly.

* 9 7 8 1 9 3 6 9 1 2 3 1 5 *